BRUCE LEE.

THE LITTLE BLACK BOOK

"MAY THE WISDOM OF THE GREATEST MINDS
BECOME YOURS."
S. C. HOLLISTER

RENEGADE PUBLISHING

TO BRUCE LEE,
THANK YOU.

CONTENTS

THE LITTLE BLACK BOOK USED TO BE A MEANS OF GETTING IN TOUCH WITH PEOPLE WHO COULD GIVE YOU WHAT YOU WANTED; MOST FAMOUSLY UNDERSTOOD AS A BOOTY CALL BOOK.

BUT, IN THIS 21ST CENTURY VERSION OF THE LITTLE BLACK BOOK, WISDOM AND KNOWLEDGE ARE THE KEY TO OPENING DOORS.

THE DESIGN OF THIS BOOK INVITES YOU TO MEDITATE ON THE WISDOM WITHIN, HAVE FOCUSED CONVERSATIONS, OR PROTECT YOUR COFFEE TABLE FROM CONDENSATION.

MAY THE WISDOM OF SOME OF THE GREATEST, BECOME YOURS.

BRUCE LEE.

THE LITTLE BLACK BOOK

Lee's Little Black Book

~

1. "Do not pray for an easy life, pray for the strength to endure a difficult one."

2. "Be like water making its way through cracks. Do not be assertive, but adjust to the object, and you shall find a way around or through it. If nothing within you stays rigid, outward things will disclose themselves."

3. "Mistakes are always forgivable, if one has the courage to admit them."

4. "A wise man can learn more from a foolish question than a fool can learn from a wise answer."

5. "Use only that which works, and take it from any place you can find it."

6. "A quick temper will make a fool of you soon enough."

7. "LOVE IS LIKE A FRIENDSHIP CAUGHT ON FIRE. IN THE BEGINNING A FLAME, VERY PRETTY, OFTEN HOT AND FIERCE, BUT STILL ONLY LIGHT AND FLICKERING. AS LOVE GROWS OLDER, OUR HEARTS MATURE AND OUR LOVE BECOMES AS COALS; DEEP-BURNING AND UNQUENCHABLE."

8. "IF YOU ALWAYS PUT LIMITS ON EVERYTHING YOU DO, PHYSICAL OR ANYTHING ELSE, IT WILL SPREAD INTO YOUR WORK AND INTO YOUR LIFE. THERE ARE NO LIMITS. THERE ARE ONLY PLATEAUS, AND YOU MUST NOT STAY THERE, YOU MUST GO BEYOND THEM."

9. "TO HELL WITH CIRCUMSTANCES; I CREATE OPPORTUNITIES."

10. "I FEAR NOT THE MAN WHO HAS PRACTICED 10,000 KICKS ONCE, BUT I FEAR THE MAN WHO HAD PRACTICED ONE KICK 10,000 TIMES."

11. "IF YOU SPEND TOO MUCH TIME THINKING ABOUT A THING, YOU'LL NEVER GET IT DONE."

12. "BE HAPPY, BUT NEVER SATISFIED."

13. "DON'T FEAR FAILURE. — NOT FAILURE,
     BUT LOW AIM, IS THE CRIME. IN GREAT
     ATTEMPTS IT IS GLORIOUS EVEN TO FAIL."

14. "A GOAL IS NOT ALWAYS MEANT TO BE
     REACHED, IT OFTEN SERVES SIMPLY AS
     SOMETHING TO AIM AT."

15. "THE DOUBTERS SAID,
     'MAN CANNOT FLY,'
     THE DOERS SAID,
     'MAYBE, BUT WE'LL TRY,'
     AND FINALLY SOARED
     IN THE MORNING GLOW
     WHILE NON-BELIEVERS
     WATCHED FROM BELOW."

16. "THE KEY TO IMMORTALITY IS FIRST
     LIVING A LIFE WORTH REMEMBERING."

17. "KNOWING IS NOT ENOUGH, WE MUST
     APPLY. WILLING IS NOT ENOUGH, WE
     MUST DO."

18. "IT IS NOT A DAILY INCREASE, BUT A
     DAILY DECREASE. HACK AWAY AT THE
     INESSENTIALS."

19. "IF YOU DON'T WANT TO SLIP UP TOMORROW, SPEAK THE TRUTH TODAY."

20. "YOU MUST BE SHAPELESS, FORMLESS, LIKE WATER. WHEN YOU POUR WATER IN A CUP, IT BECOMES THE CUP. WHEN YOU POUR WATER IN A BOTTLE, IT BECOMES THE BOTTLE. WHEN YOU POUR WATER IN A TEAPOT, IT BECOMES THE TEAPOT. WATER CAN DRIP AND IT CAN CRASH. BECOME LIKE WATER MY FRIEND."

21. "ALWAYS BE YOURSELF, EXPRESS YOURSELF, HAVE FAITH IN YOURSELF, DO NOT GO OUT AND LOOK FOR A SUCCESSFUL PERSONALITY AND DUPLICATE IT."

22. "NOTICE THAT THE STIFFEST TREE IS MOST EASILY CRACKED, WHILE THE BAMBOO OR WILLOW SURVIVES BY BENDING WITH THE WIND."

23. "THE GREAT MISTAKE IS TO ANTICIPATE THE OUTCOME OF THE ENGAGEMENT; YOU OUGHT NOT TO BE THINKING OF WHETHER IT ENDS IN VICTORY OR DEFEAT. LET NATURE TAKE ITS COURSE, AND YOUR TOOLS WILL STRIKE AT THE RIGHT MOMENT."

24. "FORGET ABOUT WINNING AND LOSING; FORGET ABOUT PRIDE AND PAIN. LET YOUR OPPONENT GRAZE YOUR SKIN AND YOU SMASH INTO HIS FLESH; LET HIM SMASH INTO YOUR FLESH AND YOU FRACTURE HIS BONES; LET HIM FRACTURE YOUR BONES AND YOU TAKE HIS LIFE! DO NOT BE CONCERNED WITH ESCAPING SAFELY - LAY YOUR LIFE BEFORE HIM!"

25. "EMPTY YOUR MIND, BE FORMLESS. SHAPELESS, LIKE WATER. IF YOU PUT WATER INTO A CUP, IT BECOMES THE CUP. YOU PUT WATER INTO A BOTTLE AND IT BECOMES THE BOTTLE. YOU PUT IT IN A TEAPOT, IT BECOMES THE TEAPOT. NOW, WATER CAN FLOW, OR IT CAN CRASH. BE WATER, MY FRIEND."

26. "AS YOU THINK, SO SHALL YOU BECOME."

27. "EMPTY YOUR CUP SO THAT IT MAY BE FILLED; BECOME DEVOID TO GAIN TOTALITY."

28. "IF THERE IS A GOD, HE IS WITHIN. YOU DON'T ASK GOD TO GIVE YOU THINGS; YOU DEPEND ON GOD FOR YOUR INNER THEME."

29. "I'M NOT IN THIS WORLD TO LIVE UP TO YOUR EXPECTATIONS, AND YOU'RE NOT IN THIS WORLD TO LIVE UP TO MINE."

30. "A GOOD TEACHER PROTECTS HIS PUPILS FROM HIS OWN INFLUENCE."

31. "FOR IT IS EASY TO CRITICIZE AND BREAK DOWN THE SPIRIT OF OTHERS, BUT TO KNOW YOURSELF TAKES A LIFETIME."

32. "IF YOU LOVE LIFE, DON'T WASTE TIME, FOR TIME IS WHAT LIFE IS MADE UP OF."

33. "TAKE THINGS AS THEY ARE. PUNCH WHEN YOU HAVE TO PUNCH. KICK WHEN YOU HAVE TO KICK."

34. "NOW I SEE THAT I WILL NEVER FIND THE LIGHT UNLESS, LIKE THE CANDLE, I AM MY OWN FUEL, CONSUMING MYSELF."

35. "TO SPEND TIME IS TO PASS IT IN A SPECIFIED MANNER. TO WASTE TIME IS TO EXPEND IT THOUGHTLESSLY OR CARELESSLY. WE ALL HAVE TIME TO EITHER SPEND OR WASTE AND IT IS OUR DECISION WHAT TO DO WITH IT. BUT ONCE PASSED, IT IS GONE FOREVER."

36. "MANY PEOPLE DEDICATE THEIR LIVES TO ACTUALIZING A CONCEPT OF WHAT THEY SHOULD BE LIKE, RATHER THAN ACTUALIZING THEMSELVES. THIS DIFFERENCE BETWEEN SELF-ACTUALIZATION AND SELF-IMAGE ACTUALIZATION IS VERY IMPORTANT. MOST PEOPLE LIVE ONLY FOR THEIR IMAGE."

37. "BE SELF-AWARE, RATHER THAN A REPETITIOUS ROBOT."

38. "USING NO WAY AS A WAY, HAVING NO LIMITATION AS LIMITATION."

39. "KNOWLEDGE EARNS YOU POWER, CHARACTER EARNS YOU RESPECT."

40. "TIME MEANS A LOT TO ME BECAUSE YOU SEE I AM ALSO A LEARNER AND AM OFTEN LOST IN THE JOY OF FOREVER DEVELOPING."

41. "DEFEAT IS NOT DEFEAT UNLESS ACCEPTED AS A REALITY-IN YOUR OWN MIND."

42. "THE MEANING OF LIFE IS THAT IT IS TO BE LIVED, AND IT IS NOT TO BE TRADED AND CONCEPTUALIZED AND SQUEEZED INTO A PATTERN OF SYSTEMS."

43. "THE SPIRIT OF THE INDIVIDUAL IS DETERMINED BY HIS DOMINATING THOUGHT HABITS."

44. "ART CALLS FOR COMPLETE MASTERY OF TECHNIQUES, DEVELOPED BY REFLECTION WITHIN THE SOUL."

45. "SHOWING OFF IS THE FOOL'S IDEA OF GLORY."

46. "THE MEANING OF LIFE IS THAT IT IS TO BE LIVED, AND IT IS NOT TO BE TRADED AND CONCEPTUALIZED AND SQUEEZED INTO A PATTERN OF SYSTEMS."

47. "THE MORE WE VALUE THINGS, THE LESS WE VALUE OURSELVES."

48. "LIFE'S BATTLES DON'T ALWAYS GO TO THE STRONGER OR FASTER MAN. BUT SOONER OR LATER THE MAN WHO WINS, IS THE MAN WHO THINKS HE CAN."

49. "Ever since I was a child I have had this instinctive urge for expansion and growth. To me, the function and duty of a quality human being is the sincere and honest development of one's potential."

50. "Don't get set into one form, adapt it and build your own, and let it grow, be like water."

51. "Boards don't hit back."

52. "The stillness in stillness is not the real stillness; only when there is stillness in movement does the universal rhythm manifest."

53. "Those who are unaware they are walking in darkness will never seek the light."

54. "Everything you do, if not in a relaxed state will be done at a lesser level than you are proficient. Thus the tensed expert marksman will aim at a level less than his/her student."

55. "The successful warrior is the average man, with laser-like focus."

56. "All knowledge leads to self-knowledge."

57. "Real living is living for others."

58. "If nothing within you stays rigid, outward things will disclose themselves. Moving, be like water. Still, be like a mirror. Respond like an echo."

59. "Self-knowledge involves relationship. To know one's self is to study one's self in action with another person."

60. "Do not deny the classical approach, simply as a reaction, or you will have created another pattern and trapped yourself there."

61. "The idea is that flowing water never goes stale, so just keep on flowing."

62. "OBEY THE PRINCIPLES WITHOUT BEING
     BOUND BY THEM."

63. "PREPARATION FOR TOMORROW IS HARD
     WORK TODAY."

64. "IT'S LIKE A FINGER POINTING AWAY TO
     THE MOON. DON'T CONCENTRATE ON
     THE FINGER OR YOU WILL MISS ALL THAT
     HEAVENLY GLORY." - STRIKING
     THOUGHTS: BRUCE LEE'S WISDOM FOR
     DAILY LIVING

65. "THE LESS EFFORT, THE FASTER AND
     MORE POWERFUL YOU WILL BE."

66. "IF YOU THINK A THING IS IMPOSSIBLE,
     YOU'LL ONLY MAKE IT IMPOSSIBLE." - TAO
     OF JEET KUNE DO

67. "YOU CANNOT FORCE THE NOW. - BUT
     CAN YOU NEITHER CONDEMN NOR
     JUSTIFY AND YET BE EXTRAORDINARILY
     ALIVE AS YOU WALK ON? YOU CAN NEVER
     INVITE THE WIND, BUT YOU MUST LEAVE
     THE WINDOW OPEN." - STRIKING
     THOUGHTS: BRUCE LEE'S WISDOM FOR
     DAILY LIVING

68. "TO ME, THE EXTRAORDINARY ASPECT OF MARTIAL ARTS LIES IN ITS SIMPLICITY. THE EASY WAY IS ALSO THE RIGHT WAY, AND MARTIAL ARTS IS NOTHING AT ALL SPECIAL; THE CLOSER TO THE TRUE WAY OF MARTIAL ARTS, THE LESS WASTAGE OF EXPRESSION THERE IS."

69. "IN BUDDHISM, THERE IS NO PLACE FOR USING EFFORT. JUST BE ORDINARY AND NOTHING SPECIAL. EAT YOUR FOOD, MOVE YOUR BOWELS, PASS WATER AND WHEN YOU'RE TIRED GO AND LIE DOWN. THE IGNORANT WILL LAUGH AT ME, BUT THE WISE WILL UNDERSTAND." - *TAO OF JEET KUNE DO*

70. "MOVING, BE LIKE WATER. STILL, BE LIKE A MIRROR. RESPOND LIKE AN ECHO."

71. "THE WORLD IS FULL OF PEOPLE WHO ARE DETERMINED TO BE SOMEBODY OR TO GIVE TROUBLE. THEY WANT TO GET AHEAD, TO STAND OUT. SUCH AMBITION HAS NO USE FOR A KUNG FU MAN, WHO REJECTS ALL FORMS OF SELF-ASSERTIVENESS AND COMPETITION." - STRIKING THOUGHTS: BRUCE LEE'S WISDOM FOR DAILY LIVING

72. "The possession of anything begins in the mind."

73. "It is compassion rather than the principle of justice which can guard us against being unjust to our fellow men." - Tao of Jeet Kune Do

74. "Linda and I aren't one and one. We are two halves that make a whole; two halves fitted together are more efficient than either half would ever be alone!"

75. "If I tell you I'm good, probably you will say I'm boasting. But if I tell you I'm not good, you'll know I'm lying."

76. "Don't think. FEEL. It's like a finger pointing at the moon. Do not concentrate on the finger, or you will miss all of the heavenly glory."

77. "Take no thought of who is right or wrong or who is better than. Be not for or against."

78. "ALL FIXED SET PATTERNS ARE INCAPABLE OF ADAPTABILITY OR PLIABILITY. THE TRUTH IS OUTSIDE OF ALL FIXED PATTERNS."

79. "THE WORD 'SUPERSTAR' IS AN ILLUSION."

80. "RELATIONSHIP IS UNDERSTANDING. IT IS A PROCESS OF SELF-REVELATION. RELATIONSHIP IS THE MIRROR IN WHICH YOU DISCOVER YOURSELF – TO BE IS TO BE RELATED." – TOA OF JEET KUNE DO

81. "ABSORB WHAT IS USEFUL, DISCARD WHAT IS USELESS AND ADD WHAT IS SPECIFICALLY YOUR OWN." - WISDOM FOR THE WAY

82. "AS LONG AS I CAN REMEMBER I FEEL I HAVE HAD THIS GREAT CREATIVE AND SPIRITUAL FORCE WITHIN ME THAT IS GREATER THAN FAITH, GREATER THAN AMBITION, GREATER THAN CONFIDENCE, GREATER THAN DETERMINATION, GREATER THAN VISION, IT IS ALL THESE COMBINED. MY BRAIN BECOMES MAGNETIZED WITH THIS DOMINATING FORCE WHICH I HOLD IN MY HAND."

83. "MAN, THE LIVING CREATURE, THE CREATING INDIVIDUAL, IS ALWAYS MORE IMPORTANT THAN ANY ESTABLISHED STYLE OR SYSTEM."

84. "YOU CAN NEVER INVITE THE WIND, BUT YOU MUST LEAVE THE WINDOW OPEN."

85. "EFFORT WITHIN THE MIND FURTHER LIMITS THE MIND, BECAUSE EFFORT IMPLIES STRUGGLE TOWARDS A GOAL AND WHEN YOU HAVE A GOAL, A PURPOSE, AN END IN VIEW, YOU HAVE PLACED A LIMIT ON THE MIND." – TAO OF JEET KUNE DO

86. "IF YOU FOLLOW THE CLASSICAL PATTERN, YOU ARE UNDERSTANDING THE ROUTINE, THE TRADITION, THE SHADOW – YOU ARE NOT UNDERSTANDING YOURSELF." ~ TAO OF JEET KUNE DO

87. "IF YOU FOLLOW THE CLASSICAL PATTERN, YOU ARE UNDERSTANDING THE ROUTINE, THE TRADITION, THE SHADOW – YOU ARE NOT UNDERSTANDING YOURSELF." ~ TOA OF JEET KUNE DO

88. "BECAUSE ONE DOES NOT WANT TO BE DISTURBED, TO BE MADE UNCERTAIN, HE ESTABLISHES A PATTERN OF CONDUCT, OF THOUGHT, A PATTERN OF RELATIONSHIP TO MAN, ETC. THEN HE BECOMES A SLAVE TO THE PATTERN AND TAKES THE PATTERN TO BE THE REAL THING."

89. "THE CONSCIOUSNESS OF SELF IS THE GREATEST HINDRANCE TO THE PROPER EXECUTION OF ALL PHYSICAL ACTION."

90. "BRING THE MIND INTO SHARP FOCUS AND MAKE IT ALERT SO THAT IT CAN IMMEDIATELY INTUIT TRUTH, WHICH IS EVERYWHERE. THE MIND MUST BE EMANCIPATED FROM OLD HABITS, PREJUDICES, RESTRICTIVE THOUGHT PROCESSES AND EVEN ORDINARY THOUGHT ITSELF." — TAO OF JEET KUNE DO

91. "JUST BE ORDINARY AND NOTHING SPECIAL. EAT YOUR FOOD, MOVE YOUR BOWELS, PASS WATER, AND WHEN YOU'RE TIRED, GO AND LIE DOWN. THE IGNORANT WILL LAUGH AT ME, BUT THE WISE WILL UNDERSTAND."

92. "DON'T GET SET INTO ONE FORM, ADAPT IT AND BUILD YOUR OWN, AND LET IT GROW, BE LIKE WATER. EMPTY YOUR MIND, BE FORMLESS, SHAPELESS — LIKE WATER. NOW YOU PUT WATER IN A CUP, IT BECOMES THE CUP; YOU PUT WATER INTO A BOTTLE IT BECOMES THE BOTTLE; YOU PUT IT IN A TEAPOT IT BECOMES THE TEAPOT. NOW WATER CAN FLOW OR IT CAN CRASH. BE WATER, MY FRIEND."

93. "YOU JUST WAIT. I'M GOING TO BE THE BIGGEST CHINESE STAR IN THE WORLD."

94. "USING NO WAY AS WAY. HAVING NO LIMITATION AS YOUR ONLY LIMITATION." — TAO OF JEET KUNE DO

95. "HAVING TOTALITY MEANS BEING CAPABLE OF FOLLOWING "WHAT IS," BECAUSE "WHAT IS" IS CONSTANTLY MOVING AND CONSTANTLY CHANGING. IF ONE IS ANCHORED TO A PARTICULAR VIEW, ONE WILL NOT BE ABLE TO FOLLOW THE SWIFT MOVEMENT OF "WHAT IS." — TAO OF JEET KUNE DO

96. "IN ORDER TO CONTROL MYSELF I MUST FIRST ACCEPT MYSELF BY GOING WITH AND NOT AGAINST MY NATURE."

97. "THE MAN WHO IS REALLY SERIOUS, WITH THE URGE TO FIND OUT WHAT TRUTH IS, HAS NO STYLE AT ALL. HE LIVES ONLY IN WHAT IS."

98. "BE LIKE WATER MAKING ITS WAY THROUGH CRACK. DO NOT BE ASSERTIVE BUT ADJUST TO THE OBJECT AND YOU SHALL FIND A WAY ROUND IT OR THROUGH IT."

99. "IF NOTHING WITHIN YOU STAYS RIGID OUTWARD THINGS WILL DISCLOSE THEMSELVES."

100. "THERE IS NO MYSTERY ABOUT MY STYLE. MY MOVEMENTS ARE SIMPLE, DIRECT AND NON-CLASSICAL. THE EXTRAORDINARY PART OF IT LIES IN ITS SIMPLICITY. EVERY MOVEMENT IN JEET KUNE-DO IS BEING SO OF ITSELF. THERE IS NOTHING ARTIFICIAL ABOUT IT. I ALWAYS BELIEVE THAT THE EASY WAY IS THE RIGHT WAY."
— TAO OF JEET KUNE DO

101. "I'M MOVING AND NOT MOVING AT ALL. I'M LIKE THE MOON UNDERNEATH THE WAVES THAT EVER GO ON ROLLING AND ROCKING. IT IS NOT, "I AM DOING THIS," BUT RATHER, AN INNER REALIZATION THAT "THIS IS HAPPENING THROUGH ME," OR "IT IS DOING THIS FOR ME." THE CONSCIOUSNESS OF SELF IS THE GREATEST HINDRANCE TO THE PROPER EXECUTION OF ALL PHYSICAL ACTION." — TAO OF JEET KUNE DO

102. "REMEMBER NO MAN IS REALLY DEFEATED UNLESS HE IS DISCOURAGED."

103. "VOIDNESS IS THAT WHICH STANDS RIGHT IN THE MIDDLE BETWEEN THIS AND THAT. THE VOID IS ALL-INCLUSIVE, HAVING NO OPPOSITE--THERE IS NOTHING WHICH IT EXCLUDES OR OPPOSES. IT IS LIVING VOID, BECAUSE ALL FORMS COME OUT OF IT AND WHOEVER REALIZES THE VOID IS FILLED WITH LIFE AND POWER AND THE LOVE OF ALL BEINGS." — TAO OF JEET KUNE DO

104. "IN THE MIDDLE OF CHAOS LIES OPPORTUNITY."

105. "ONLY THE SELF-SUFFICIENT STAND ALONE - MOST PEOPLE FOLLOW THE CROWD AND IMITATE."

106. "PRACTICE MAKES PERFECT. AFTER A LONG TIME OF PRACTICING, OUR WORK WILL BECOME NATURAL, SKILLFUL, SWIFT, AND STEADY."

107. "SATORI - IN THE AWAKENING FROM A DREAM. AWAKENING AND SELF-REALIZATION AND SEEING INTO ONE'S OWN BEING - THESE ARE SYNONYMOUS." — STRIKING THOUGHTS: BRUCE LEE'S WISDOM FOR DAILY LIVING

108. "...GOOD TECHNIQUE INCLUDES QUICK CHANGES, GREAT VARIETY AND SPEED. IT MAY BE A SYSTEM OF REVERSALS MUCH LIKE A CONCEPT OF GOD AND THE DEVIL. IN THE SPEED OF EVENTS, WHICH ONE IS REALLY IN CHARGE?...TO PUT THE HEART OF MARTIAL ARTS IN YOUR OWN HEART AND HAVE IT BE A PART OF YOU MEANS TOTAL COMPREHENSION AND THE USE OF A FREE STYLE. WHEN YOU HAVE THAT YOU WILL KNOW THAT THERE ARE NO LIMITS." — TAO OF JEET KUNE DO

109. "In Life There are No Limits, Only Plateaus."

110. "Defeat is a state of mind; no one is ever defeated until defeat has been accepted as a reality."

111. "Give up thinking as though not giving it up. Observe techniques as though not observing." — Tao of Jeet Kune Do

112. "To see a thing uncolored by one's own personal preferences and desires is to see it in its own pristine simplicity." — Tao of Jeet Kune Do

113. "if you want to be immortal live a life worth remembering"

114. "Do not allow negative thoughts to enter your mind for they are the weeds that strange confidence."

115. "Jeet Kune Do, you see, has no definite lines or boundaries – only those you make yourself." — Tao of Jeet Kune Do

116. "THE ATTITUDE, 'YOU CAN WIN IF YOU WANT TO BADLY ENOUGH,' MEANS THAT THE WILL TO WIN IS CONSTANT. NO AMOUNT OF PUNISHMENT, NO AMOUNT OF EFFORT, NO CONDITION IS TOO 'TOUGH' TO TAKE IN ORDER TO WIN. SUCH AN ATTITUDE CAN BE DEVELOPED ONLY IF WINNING IS CLOSELY TIED TO THE PRACTITIONER'S IDEALS AND DREAMS." — TAO OF JEET KUNE DO

117. "IT IS NOT A SHAME TO BE KNOCKED DOWN BY OTHER PEOPLE. THE IMPORTANT THING IS TO ASK WHEN YOU'RE BEING KNOCKED DOWN, 'WHY AM I BEING KNOCKED DOWN?' IF A PERSON CAN REFLECT IN THIS WAY, THEN THERE IS HOPE FOR THIS PERSON."

118. "PUT 'GOING THE EXTRA MILE' TO WORK AS PART OF ONE'S DAILY HABIT."

119. "THE IDEAL IS UNNATURAL NATURALNESS, OR NATURAL UNNATURALNESS. I MEAN IT IS A COMBINATION OF BOTH. I MEAN HERE IS NATURAL INSTINCT AND HERE IS CONTROL. YOU ARE TO COMBINE THE TWO IN HARMONY."

120. "THE PERFECT WAY IS ONLY DIFFICULT FOR THOSE WHO PICK AND CHOOSE. DO NOT LIKE, DO NOT DISLIKE; ALL WILL THEN BE CLEAR. MAKE A HAIRBREADTH DIFFERENCE AND HEAVEN AND EARTH ARE SET APART; IF YOU WANT THE TRUTH TO STAND CLEAR BEFORE YOU, NEVER BE FOR OR AGAINST. THE STRUGGLE BETWEEN "FOR" AND "AGAINST" IS THE MIND'S WORST DISEASE." — TAO OF JEET KUNE DO

121. "BE FLUID LIKE WATER."

122. "I FEAR NOT THE MAN THAT CAN THROW A THOUSAND DIFFERENT KICKS ONCE, BUT THE MAN WHO CAN THROW ONE KICK A THOUSAND TIMES."

123. "BE LIKE WATER MAKING ITS WAY THROUGH CRACKS. DO NOT BE ASSERTIVE, BUT ADJUST TO THE OBJECT, AND YOU SHALL FIND A WAY ROUND OR THROUGH IT. IF NOTHING WITHIN YOU STAYS RIGID, OUTWARD THINGS WILL DISCLOSE THEMSELVES."

124. "MY STYLE? YOU CAN CALL IT THE ART OF FIGHTING WITHOUT FIGHTING."

125. "EMPTY YOUR MIND, BE FORMLESS. SHAPELESS, LIKE WATER. IF YOU PUT WATER INTO A CUP, IT BECOMES THE CUP. YOU PUT WATER INTO A BOTTLE AND IT BECOMES THE BOTTLE. YOU PUT IT IN A TEAPOT IT BECOMES THE TEAPOT. NOW, WATER CAN FLOW OR IT CAN CRASH. BE WATER MY FRIEND."

126. "WHAT YOU MUST NOT DO NOW IS TO WORRY AND THINK OF THE NATIONALS THAT IS NOW OF THE PAST. WHAT YOU HABITUALLY THINK LARGELY DETERMINES WHAT YOU WILL BECOME. REMEMBER, SUCCESS IS A JOURNEY, NOT A DESTINATION. I HAVE FAITH IN YOUR ABILITY. YOU WILL DO JUST FINE." — LETTERS OF THE DRAGON

127. "IF YOU TRULY LOVE LIFE, DON'T WASTE TIME BECAUSE TIME IS WHAT LIFE IS MADE OF."

128. "ART REACHES ITS GREATEST PEAK WHEN DEVOID OF SELF-CONSCIOUSNESS. FREEDOM DISCOVERS MAN THE MOMENT HE LOSES CONCERN OVER WHAT IMPRESSION HE IS MAKING OR ABOUT TO MAKE."

129. "THERE IS "WHAT IS" ONLY WHEN THERE IS NO COMPARING AND TO LIVE WITH "WHAT IS" IS TO BE PEACEFUL." — TAO OF JEET KUNE DO

130. "NEVER TROUBLE TROUBLE TILL TROUBLE TROUBLES YOU. I'LL NOT WILLINGLY OFFEND, NOR BE EASILY OFFENDED."

131. "WE HAVE GREAT WORK AHEAD OF US, AND IT NEEDS DEVOTION AND MUCH, MUCH ENERGY. TO GROW, TO DISCOVER, WE NEED INVOLVEMENT, WHICH IS SOMETHING I EXPERIENCE EVERY DAY – SOMETIMES GOOD, SOMETIMES FRUSTRATING. NO MATTER WHAT, YOU MUST LET YOUR INNER LIGHT GUIDE YOU OUT OF THE DARKNESS."

132. "I WISH NEITHER TO POSSESS NOR TO BE POSSESSED. I NO LONGER COVET 'PARADISE'. MORE IMPORTANT, I NO LONGER FEAR 'HELL'."

133. "EMOTION CAN BE THE ENEMY, IF YOU GIVE INTO YOUR EMOTION, YOU LOSE YOURSELF. YOU MUST BE AT ONE WITH YOUR EMOTIONS, BECAUSE THE BODY ALWAYS FOLLOWS THE MIND."

134. "SHOWING OFF IS THE FOOL'S IDEA OF GLORY."

135. "IF YOU WANT TO LEARN TO SWIM JUMP INTO THE WATER. ON DRY LAND NO FRAME OF MIND IS EVER GOING TO HELP YOU."

136. "THE MARTIAL ARTS ARE BASED UPON UNDERSTANDING, HARD WORK AND A TOTAL COMPREHENSION OF SKILLS. POWER TRAINING AND THE USE OF FORCE ARE EASY, BUT TOTAL COMPREHENSION OF ALL OF THE SKILLS OF THE MARTIAL ARTS IS VERY DIFFICULT TO ACHIEVE." — TAO OF JEET KUNE DO: NEW EXPANDED EDITION

137. "TO UNDERSTAND TECHNIQUES, YOU MUST LEARN THAT THEY CONTAIN A LOT OF CONDENSED MOVEMENT." — TAO OF JEET KUNE DO: NEW EXPANDED EDITION

138. "WHEN THE OPPONENT EXPANDS, I CONTRACT. WHEN HE CONTRACTS, I EXPAND. AND, WHEN THERE IS AN OPPORTUNITY, I DO NOT HIT - IT HITS ALL BY ITSELF."

139. "IF YOU SPEND TOO MUCH TIME THINKING ABOUT A THING YOU WILL NEVER GET IT DONE."

140. "SERIOUSLY, IF YOU ALWAYS PUT LIMITS ON WHAT YOU CAN DO, PHYSICAL OR ANYTHING ELSE; IT'LL SPREAD OVER INTO THE REST OF YOUR LIFE. IT'LL SPREAD INTO YOUR WORK, INTO YOUR MORALITY, INTO YOUR ENTIRE BEING... THERE ARE NO LIMITS. THERE ARE PLATEAUS, BUT YOU MUST NOT STAY THERE, YOU MUST GO BEYOND THEM. IF IT KILLS YOU, IT KILLS YOU. A MAN MUST CONSTANTLY EXCEED HIS LEVEL."

141. "IF YOU SPEND TOO MUCH TIME THINKING ABOUT A THING, YOU'LL NEVER GET IT DONE. MAKE AT LEAST ONE DEFINITE MOVE DAILY TOWARD YOU GOAL."

142. "DO NOT PRAY FOR AN EASY LIFE, PRAY FOR THE STRENGTH TO ENDURE THE DIFFICULT ONE."

...

MORE TITLES IN *THE LITTLE BLACK BOOK* SERIES:

IF THERE IS SOMEONE YOU'D LIKE TO SEE ADDED TO *THE LITTLE BLACK BOOK* SERIES, PLEASE LEAVE A COMMENT IN THIS BOOKS REVIEW SECTION ON AMAZON.COM.

Made in the USA
Lexington, KY
18 November 2015